The Pros and Cons of
WIND POWER
Richard and Louise Spilsbury

New York

Published in 2008 by The Rosen Publishing Group, Inc.
29 East 21st Street, New York, NY 10010

First Edition

Series Editor: Jennifer Schofield
Editor: Susie Brooks
Consultant: Rob Bowden
Designer: Jane Hawkins
Cover designer: Paul Cherrill
Picture Researcher: Diana Morris
Illustrator: Ian Thompson
Indexer: Sue Lightfoot

Picture Acknowledgments:
Joerg Boethling/Still Pictures: 38. Martin Bond/SPL: 14.
Jon Bower/Ecoscene: 33. Steven Clevenger/Corbis: 12.
Phillip Colla/Ecoscene: front cover. dpa/Corbis; 17.
EASI Images: 25, 36. Warren Faidley/Corbis: front cover br, 45.
Patricia Fen/Photographers Direct: 26. Pat Groves/Ecoscene: 19.
Ian Harwood/Ecoscene: 6. Michael Mottlau/Polfoto/Topfoto: 35.
Jörg Müller/Photographers Direct: 29. Russell Munson/Corbis: 1, 21.
Courtesy of Quiet Revolution: 40. Spectrum Photofile/Photographers
Direct: 42. Courtesy of Vestas Wind Systems A/S: 22, 30.

Library of Congress Cataloging-in-Publication Data
Spilsbury, Richard, 1963-
  the pros and cons of Wind power / Richard and Louise Spilsbury. -- 1st ed.
     p. cm. -- (The energy debate)
  Includes index.
  ISBN-13: 978-1-4042-3745-2 (library binding)
  ISBN-10: 1-4042-3745-3 (library binding)
  1. Wind power plants--Juvenile literature. 2.
Wind power plants--Environmental aspects--Juvenile literature.
I. Spilsbury, Louise. II. Title.
  TK1541.S65 2007
  621.31'2136--dc22

Manufactured in China

Contents

CHAPTER 1 Wind power and the energy debate

There is worldwide debate about how we can provide the energy we need now and in the future. As traditional resources are stretched and populations grow, more and more, people are looking to alternative sources of power. One source of energy we can use is moving air. Wind power is attracting interest across the globe.

World of energy

People rely on energy to run vehicles, power industries, and to generate electricity. The major source of energy for humans is heat from burning fuels. Wood was probably the first fuel ever used, but since the eighteenth century, people in more economically developed countries (MEDCs) have relied mostly on fossil fuels. Fossil fuels, such as coal, oil, and natural gas, are the remains of plants and animals that lived millions of years ago. Like plants today, they trapped the Sun's energy to live and grow. Burning fossil fuels releases this stored energy. Most power stations use fossil fuels to heat up water and create high-pressure steam. The moving steam turns machines that generate electricity.

The world's growing population uses more enormous quantities of electricity every year. People's

> " It is evident that the fortunes of the world's human population, for better or for worse, are inextricably interrelated with the use that is made of energy resources. "
>
> M. King Hubbert, U.S. geophysicist, *Resources and Man*, 1969

expectations of what they need to live in comfort are also changing worldwide. As consumers buy more and more electrical appliances, from computers and televisions, to washing machines and air conditioning, so the demand for energy rises.

Looming crises

Unfortunately, all fossil fuels are running out—they are nonrenewable, which means they cannot be replaced. Scientists estimate that many reserves of oil and natural gas will run out in less than 50 years if we use them up at predicted rates—and although there is still enough coal to last for several hundred years, it, too, is in limited supply. Experts predict an energy crisis unless we find alternative sources.

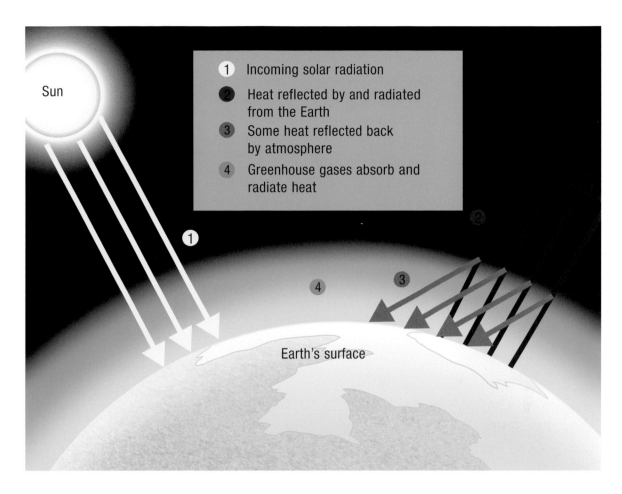

Fossil fuels are also creating environmental crises. Burning these fuels releases enormous quantities of gases such as carbon dioxide (CO_2), and tiny particles, into the air. Not only do these pollute the air, causing health problems and harmful acid rain, but they also contribute to the greenhouse effect and global warming. Many scientists agree that the growing layer of these greenhouse gases in the Earth's atmosphere is trapping the Sun's heat sufficiently to increase temperatures and change the climate in significant ways around the world.

△ Increasing greenhouse gases in the atmosphere prevent more heat from escaping the Earth.

Renewable future

These problems have driven people to think about using renewable energy sources. Some industries and homes are burning alternatives to fossil fuels, such as biogas produced from household or crop waste. People are also making use of free energy, such as light and heat from the Sun, and wind power. Renewable energy sources will not run out, and create little or no pollution.

Putting wind to work

Using wind as an energy source is not a new idea. Boats and ships powered by sails that catch the wind have been around since Ancient Egyptian times, over 5,000 years ago. Records of the earliest machines directly driven by the wind exist from over 2,000 years ago. Windmills, with sails turning heavy millstones to grind grain into flour, were invented in Persia (present-day Iran) in 200 BC. Wind pumps, using moving sails to pump water from underground wells, developed in China around the same time. Merchants and traders who traveled in Asia brought these ideas

▽ Wind turbines and fossil fuel power stations, seen here together in Wales, are both part of the energy mix. However, their contributions to pollution and climate change are very different.

to Europe, where they spread. Wind pumps and windmills were still in widespread use up until the early twentieth century. It is only since the end of the nineteenth century that wind energy has been captured to generate electricity.

Why wind power?

Wind turbines became more widely used to produce electricity in the last quarter of the twentieth century, when fossil fuels rose in price (see page 13). In isolated communities without easy access to an electricity network, or grid, wind power can be a cheap solution to people's electricity needs.

Another reason wind and other renewable energy sources are more popular today is that people are experiencing the effects of climate change and want to stop it. Gradually rising temperatures are shrinking the polar ice caps and threatening the survival of many rare species of wildlife that have adapted to particular habitats. Changing weather patterns are causing droughts and forest fires in some areas, and flooding and landslides in others. There are international agreements between many countries, such as the United Nations Kyoto protocol (see page 36), to limit the quantities of greenhouse gases they release into the atmosphere. One way to achieve this is by using renewables.

> **" The bottom of the oil barrel is now visible. "**
>
> Christopher Flavin, *Worldwatch*, July 1985

The energy mix

People around the globe get their electricity from a mix of different sources. Coal- and gas-fired power stations create almost two-thirds of all the electricity used in the world. The next major contributors are nuclear power, which harnesses the strong forces inside atoms to produce heat, and hydropower, which uses the energy in moving water. At present other renewables, including wind power and biomass power, are minor players in the mix.

However, the types of renewable energy most prominent in the energy mix in any country or region depend on a variety of factors. For example, hydropower is common in Nepal, because meltwater from its high mountains feeds many rushing rivers. Wind power is significant in Germany, not only because it is windy, but also because the government promotes and subsidizes it. Solar power stations are being developed in Egypt, because this country gets lots of sunshine each day.

CHAPTER 2 | How does wind power work?

Converting the wind's energy into electricity is not just a matter of putting up a turbine. Consideration must be given to how, when, and where winds happen, to get the positioning right. Wind turbines are complex machines that vary in design for different generation situations.

The source of wind

Wind is the name for movements of air in the atmosphere, mainly caused by the Sun. Chemical reactions in the Sun release huge amounts of light and heat energy, and some of this radiates through 93 million miles (150 million kilometers) of space to reach the Earth. The Sun's heat warms air above the Earth by different amounts. This depends partly on the curved shape of our planet—the poles are much colder than the equator, because they are farther from the Sun—and on the time of day and year, because the Earth spins around both its axis and the Sun.

Air molecules spread out as they become warmer. This makes warm air less dense than colder air, so it rises upward. Denser, colder air flows into the gaps left behind. Warm areas of air have low pressure, and colder areas have high pressure. Winds always blow from high- to low-pressure areas.

Predictable winds

Winds blow in predictable patterns. Areas of high pressure at the poles and low pressure at the Equator should create winds constantly blowing toward the equator. However, the Earth's constant rotation sends the winds off course. For example, trade winds blow from around 30° latitude toward the equator from the northeast in the northern hemisphere, and from a southeasterly direction in the southern hemisphere.

Some winds are determined by topography (the lie of the land) and geography. With increasing altitude, air becomes colder, but also has lower pressure than air nearer sea level. This means that strong winds often blow on mountains and high land. Air above the oceans takes longer to warm and cool than air above land, so this causes predictable winds in coastal regions. For example, the monsoon wind blows from the cool, high-pressure Indian ocean onto the hotter, lower-pressure land, bringing with it vast quantities of rain.

Wind speeds

Wind speeds are fastest when pressure differences are greatest. People may describe slow winds as breezes and

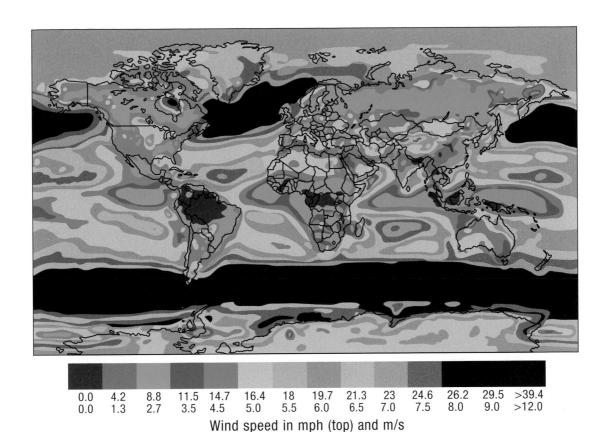

| 0.0 | 4.2 | 8.8 | 11.5 | 14.7 | 16.4 | 18 | 19.7 | 21.3 | 23 | 24.6 | 26.2 | 29.5 | >39.4 |
| 0.0 | 1.3 | 2.7 | 3.5 | 4.5 | 5.0 | 5.5 | 6.0 | 6.5 | 7.0 | 7.5 | 8.0 | 9.0 | >12.0 |

Wind speed in mph (top) and m/s

faster ones as gales, but meteorologists compare wind speed accurately using anemometers. These are miniwindmills whose speed of rotation is converted into miles per hour (mph), meters per second (m/s), feet per second (ft/s), and other units. The Beaufort scale,

△ This map shows how wind energy resources vary across the Earth.

developed in 1806 by a British Navy admiral, estimates wind force based on observations of its effects. It is still used to compare wind speeds worldwide.

A Shortened Beaufort Scale

Force	Description	Effects	Wind speed mph (kph)
0	Calm	Smoke rises vertically	0 (0)
3	Gentle breeze	Leaves in constant motion	7–12 (12–19)
6	Strong breeze	Large branches in motion	25-31 (40–50)
8	Fresh gale	Breaks twigs off trees; impedes walking	38-46 (62–74)
12	Hurricane	Widespread damage occurs	74+ (119+)

The wind turbine

A wind turbine is a machine for converting the kinetic energy, or movement, of wind into electrical energy. The most obvious moving part of any wind turbine is the rotor. This usually has two or three blades mounted at angles of around 45° on a central hub. The rotor generally faces the oncoming wind and is designed to adjust when wind direction changes.

In cross section, each blade is shaped aerodynamically, like an airplane wing. When wind hits the front of each blade, differences in the shapes of curves forming the front and back

▽ The nacelle can move from side to side on the tower to point the turbine hub toward the wind. Each blade can twist to make sure the hub rotates at the right speed in differing wind conditions.

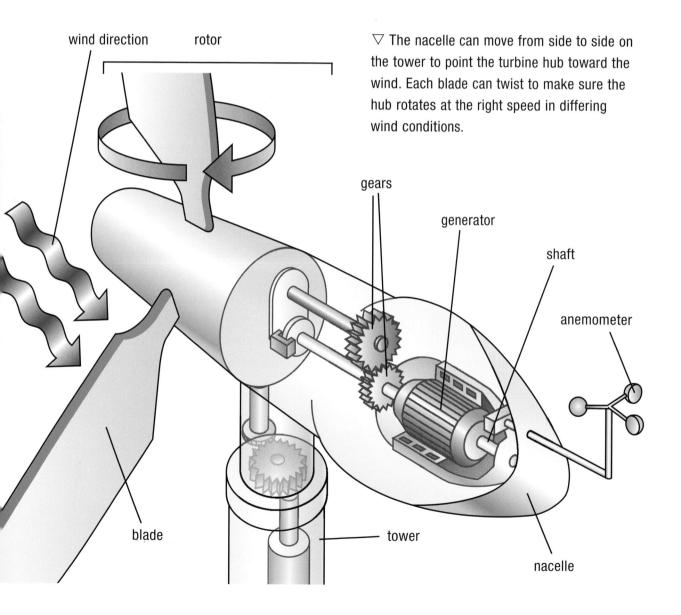

wind direction   rotor

gears

generator

shaft

anemometer

blade

tower

nacelle

of the blade create variations in the speed that air moves over them. This causes pressure differences, making the blade lift and pushing it around to the side. The rotor spins on a shaft inside a covered box called the *nacelle*. The nacelle is set on top of a concrete or steel tower. This raises the blades high above the ground, where winds blow with more force than lower down.

Making electricity

Inside the nacelle, the shaft is linked to a gearbox that turns a generator – the part of the turbine that creates electricity. Wind hitting the rotor typically makes the shaft revolve about 20–30 times each minute. This is not fast enough to operate the generator. The gearbox contains a series of interconnected cogs with different numbers of teeth. When a cog with many teeth connects to a second cog with fewer teeth, the second one moves faster than the first. The right combination of cogs in a wind turbine increases the rotational speed inside the gearbox. The final cog in the gearbox is connected to a second, high-speed shaft that typically turns about 50 times faster than the first.

A set of tightly wound copper wire coils is attached to the high-speed shaft. The shaft spins inside a circle of magnets. As the coils pass each magnet, they cause electrons to move back and forth in the wires. The fast movement of electrons is *electricity*, or electrical energy that can do work. The power output of wind turbines is usually measured in kilowatt hours (kW) or megawatt hours (MW), which means thousands or millions of watts generated per hour.

Distribution

Electricity flows away from the generator through power cables in the turbine tower. In some cases, the power is used on-site, but in other cases, it enters a transformer. This is a machine that increases the voltage of electrical energy, which is like giving it an extra push, so it can travel through the electrical grid. The grid is a vast network of cables, many supported on pylons, which takes power to homes and businesses long distances away.

> ❝ I am busy just now again on electromagnetism, and think I have got hold of a good thing, but can't say. It may be a weed instead of a fish that, after all my labor, I may at last pull up. ❞
>
> Michael Faraday (1791–1867), British inventor of the earliest generator, the dynamo

Early wind turbines

Wind turbines have been used to generate electricity for more than a century. In 1887, the first large windmill designed especially for this purpose was built by Charles F. Brush in the grounds of his mansion in Ohio. The windmill had a circular rotor 56 feet (17 meters) wide made from 144 cedarwood blades. It could produce 12 kW of electricity to charge the batteries that powered his mansion's lights. In the 1890s, experiments by the Danish meteorologist, Poul la Cour, developed turbines further. He found out that fast-moving rotors with fewer blades could produce more power. By 1908, turbines with four blades could generate up to 25 kW.

In the 1930s, especially in the U.S., small multibladed turbines became popular on farms in the countryside, where mains electricity was unavailable. These turbines were cheap and easy to set up. The first large turbine to deliver electricity to a local

◁ This view at the Colorado Green Wind Project shows wind power old and new. In the foreground is a small multibladed windpump of the past; standing behind it is a modern giant wind turbine.

electricity grid started operating in 1941 on a mountain in Vermont. This enormous turbine produced 1.25 MW using twin steel blades, each about 98 feet (30 meters) long.

Postwar changes

The spread of wind power slowed and finally ground to a halt during and after World War II (1939–1945). The war effort used any available steel to make ammunition and military vehicles. This meant that additional steel turbines could not be built, nor could existing ones be repaired. When the war finished, fossil fuels dropped in price. The U.S. and other countries built national grids, distributing electricity from giant coal-fired power stations. This power was cheaper than wind power. Some postwar governments built nuclear power plants. Having seen the devastating power of nuclear bombs dropped on Japan, many people recognized the great potential of making cheap nuclear power. However, there were considerable safety concerns.

Increased awareness

By the 1980s, interest reawakened in wind power as oil prices rose. This was because less oil was being sold by countries in the major producing region on Earth—the Middle East. Manufacturers came up with different turbines that could generate cheap, plentiful electricity. One of the most important of these was the three-bladed 55 kW Nordtank turbine.

The Nordtank design could be made in pieces in factories and assembled on-site. The cost of wind power per kilowatt hour halved compared to previous turbines. Using modern materials, such as cast, reinforced concrete, designs like the Nordtank were gradually scaled up in size to create more power. The biggest turbines of today have a rotor circumference of around 394 feet (120 meters)—almost as big as the London Eye—and can output 5 MW.

> "The great wind turbine on a Vermont mountain proved that men could build a practical machine, which would synchronously generate electricity in large quantities by means of wind power... And it proved that at some future time, homes may be illuminated, and factories may be powered, by this new means."
>
> Vannevar Bush, dean of engineering, Massachusetts Institute of Technology, 1946

Turbine designs

Currently, of all turbine types, horizontal axis wind turbines (HAWTs) are by far the most common. These propeller-style turbines have rotors that turn in a vertical plane. Almost all HAWTs have an odd number of blades, usually three but rarely one, to enhance stability. When wind pushes against the blades, it presses the tips backward. This effect is strongest on the highest blade, facing the most forceful wind, and weakest on the lowest, because the tower right behind it deflects the wind, causing wind shade (see page 20). Two-bladed rotors are rare, because differences in the force on the blades make them unstable.

▽ These turbines are Darrieus VAWTs (vertical axis wind turbines) at an experimental power plant in Canada. They need guide wires to hold them up.

The nacelle is designed to pivot on its tower, because HAWTs generate best when they face the wind directly. Smaller, lighter nacelles pivot using a tail fan, which is a small, additional rotor or rudder at right angles to the main one. A wind blowing from the side pushes against the fan, turning the nacelle on the tower. Larger turbines have strong motors that turn the heavy nacelle, using data from a wind vane positioned on top of the nacelle.

A different axis

Vertical axis wind turbines (VAWTs) have blades that move around in the horizontal plane, mounted on an upright shaft. They have no nacelle, since the gearbox and generator are positioned at ground level. VAWTs can work in wind from different directions. They come in two styles. The Savonius design is a little like an anemometer, with cups to catch the wind mounted in opposite directions on different sides, and is an inefficient turbine. The Darrieus design (see opposite), which originated in France in 1927, is sometimes described as looking like an eggbeater, with two or three c-shaped or vertical blades mounted on its shaft. This design can generate power in weak winds at ground level, but it is unstable higher up. This is because its long blades tend to vibrate in stronger winds, making the shaft wobble, unless it has sturdy supporting cables.

THE ARGUMENT: One turbine type is better than the other

HORIZONTAL AXIS
For:
- HAWTs operate at a wide range of wind speeds and generate high levels of power.
- Rotors are out of the way in the air.

Against:
- Turbines need to be pointed in the direction of prevailing wind, which varies at different times.
- Towers are expensive to erect, and nacelle parts are tricky to maintain.

VERTICAL AXIS
For:
- VAWTs work in any wind direction, with no need for a tall tower.
- Gears and generators at ground level are easier to maintain.

Against:
- They can operate only in slow winds and generate low power.
- They need a push to get started and are unstable at high speed.

Harvesting wind energy

We can think of wind as a resource a little like a farmer's crops. Farmers with more land can harvest more. The amount of wind a turbine can harvest increases the longer the blades are, because the area of air the rotor sweeps through gets bigger. For example, doubling the blade length produces a swept area four times bigger, and the turbine generates four times as much power.

The weather has an impact on wind power just as it does on crops. A small difference in wind speed dramatically affects the wind harvest. For example, an increase in wind speed from 16 feet (5 meters) per second to 20 feet (6 meters) per second almost doubles the power created. Taller towers position rotors in faster wind than at ground level. Doubling altitude increases wind power by around one-third. Given these statistics, should all turbines be very tall with gigantic blades?

The right size

Any turbine needs to be the right size for its situation. This is partly to do with efficiency. For example, in places with weaker wind, there would not be enough force to turn a giant rotor and the large generator it operates. In places with strong winds, small turbines would not harvest enough of the resource. They may even turn so fast that the gearbox and generator overheat or the rotor is damaged. All modern HAWTs have inbuilt safety features in the nacelle, including brakes on the shafts and motors, to twist the blades so that they catch less wind. Turbine size is also critically affected by cost and design. Bigger blades and towers cost much more to make, transport, and build on-site than smaller ones. Longer blades are heavier and flex more than shorter ones, so they are more likely to bend, or even snap as they rotate.

New blades

In the past, the only materials available for making blades were wood and steel. Modern materials that are light, strong, and stiff allow turbine designers to make longer blades today. However, any blade design needs to be tested before being put into operation. Blades are usually made of layers of fiberglass or carbon fiber stuck together with plastic. For testing, a blade is clamped horizontally in a heavy concrete block, and made to flap up and down for about three months using electric motors. This mimics the stresses it would face when rotating in different wind speeds. During the test, designers can assess whether the blade layers are coming apart. They use infrared cameras to detect buildup of heat in the blade, which can indicate breaking fibers.

▽ The gigantic blades on turbines, such as this Repower 5M,
which stands 600 feet (183 meters) tall, dwarf the vehicles below. All parts
of a turbine have to be carefully tested before assembly.

CHAPTER 3 Wind power in practice

Wind power is used worldwide in a range of scales and settings. Resources vary, from small, single turbines that provide private power for individuals, to groupings of giant turbines that harvest strong sea winds.

Microgeneration

Microgeneration is the generation of electricity, by renewable means, for individuals or small groups. Small-scale wind turbines are often used for microgeneration along with solar cells. They are easy to set up and need wind speeds of more than only 13 feet (4 meters) per second to work efficiently.

A small wind turbine with a rotor 3 feet (1 meter) wide, weighing 33 pounds (15 kilos), can generate half a kilowatt per hour. This is enough to charge batteries in yachts, canal boats, vans, and other low-powered vehicles, but is not enough to supply a house with power. During one year, a three-bedroom house in a MEDC uses at least 5 MW, for everything from lighting and heating, to washing machines and computers. A turbine to generate this much power needs a rotor 10–16 feet (3–5 meters) across and needs to be mounted above 33 feet (10 meters) in the air to catch stronger winds. Small turbines are sometimes used in isolated, windy settings where there is no electricity grid—for example, to power lighting on a remote mountain railroad platform. They are also used in densely populated urban settings, on top of tall buildings and schools, to supplement existing power supplies.

Setting up micro projects

People who want to install small turbines for private use can rarely just go out and buy one. They need to contact specialist suppliers who can also advise, for example, on whether their wind resource is adequate, or where to site the turbine. Apart from a turbine, users need other things— for example, permission to put the machine up, as well as specialist electrical equipment, such as the right cabling and power convertors, so the electricity generated can be used.

> " The ability to produce clean, green energy from homes or businesses can help to lessen our carbon emissions and bring down fuel bills. "
>
> Malcolm Wicks, U.K. energy minister

△ In this remote rural area in Scotland, microgeneration by wind is a major source of electricity.

CASE STUDY:
The coldest wind power on Earth

Antarctic winds are the strongest and coldest anywhere on Earth. The high-pressure cold air sinking over the South Pole forces out high-speed, subzero winds at up to 230 feet per second (70 meters per second). Before 2003, scientists at Australia's Mawson Antarctic research station generated all their electricity by burning oil—but they then decided to install two 300 kW wind turbines. The turbines are designed to survive extreme conditions in the Antarctic. For example, they have heated blades to help stop heavy ice from building up on them and making them unstable. They also have no gearboxes, which could potentially freeze. By 2006, the turbines were generating up to 80 percent of the station's electricity.

Wind on the grid

Wind turbines do not have to be massive to generate large enough amounts of electricity to add to the power grid. Instead, several medium-sized turbines can be grouped together in a wind farm. For example, ten 1.5 MW turbines together in a farm generate as much as three giant 5 MW units. The advantage is that each smaller turbine is much cheaper to buy and will run at slower wind speeds.

Wind power is described as modular. If a wind farm needs to generate more power, if a community is growing, for example, additional turbine modules can be added to those already there.

The importance of spacing

The careful design of a wind farm is crucial if its turbines are to work properly. Rotors extract energy from the wind, so it makes sense that air leaving the turbine has less energy than that blowing against the rotor. The space behind a turbine is known as *wind shade*. Air in the wind shade mixes with higher-energy air around it, causing swirling air movements in variable directions. This is a type of turbulence. Turbulence also occurs to the sides of the rotor. Further turbulence is caused by obstacles to the wind around turbines, such as trees, rocks, or buildings, which stall winds or make them veer off course.

CASE STUDY:
Farming trade winds in Jamaica

The West Indian island of Jamaica has to import oil to fuel most of its power stations. However, rising costs have doubled the country's oil bill since 1998. This uses up money from tourism that could be spent on development for Jamaican people, and it makes electricity very expensive. Trade winds that blow across Jamaica almost year-round have the potential to provide some of the island's power at cheaper prices. The Wigton Wind Farm was built in 2004, on windy wasteland around mountain mines in Jamaica. The farm has 27 wind turbines, each rated at 750 kW, generating a total of 20 MW. These are spread out in a row at 328-foot (100-meter) intervals along high ridges to avoid turbulence. The company that operates Wigton plans to open more wind farms with a similar design in the future.

In order to avoid turbulence completely, turbines should be as far apart as possible. However, there is often a need to use as little space as possible, because it can be expensive to buy or hire land to put turbines on, and to install cables to link them together. Turbines in a typical wind farm are usually spaced 5–9 rotor diameters in front of, or behind, one another, and 3–5 rotor diameters apart side by side, to reduce turbulence to minimal levels.

> **"** A good rule of thumb is that a single square kilometer of land can support 10–15 MW of wind power. **"**
>
> New Zealand Wind Energy Association, 2006

▽ This regular wind farm layout in California looks spectacular from the air.

All at sea

Offshore wind farms are groups of turbines with towers secured to the bottom of the ocean. Given the extra costs involved in transporting turbines out to sea and the difficulties of building deep underwater, why are offshore developments increasing? The main reason is the quality of the wind resource. A look out to sea confirms that ocean surfaces are essentially flat.

△ A powerful tug boat with a tall crane was needed to erect this offshore wind turbine in Scroby Sands, U.K.

Winds blow harder offshore and with less turbulence at lower altitude, because they are uninterrupted by obstacles, such as hills and buildings. Therefore, offshore turbines need towers just high enough to raise the turning blades above the water.

It is estimated that offshore turbines use a third more of the wind energy blowing past them than onshore ones, mainly because turbulence is less.

A second important advantage of offshore wind power is space. It is no surprise that there are more offshore wind farms in Europe, where land is crowded and expensive to buy, than in the U.S., which has an overall lower density of population. Offshore turbines can have much bigger blades, and therefore generate more power, partly because there is more space available in which they can turn.

The right support

Offshore turbines need stronger supports than onshore turbines, because their towers have to withstand the power of waves—a power that increases with water depth. Onshore towers are generally screwed into deep, heavy foundations made from poured concrete. However, concrete foundations are difficult to make at sea and very expensive to tow out to the wind farm site. As a result, most offshore turbines have hollow steel bases—a tenth of the weight of concrete foundations—which are positioned on the sea floor and then filled with heavy material to weigh them down. Those in deepest water have the tower driven deep into the sea floor, or stabilized by a vast underwater tripod. Difficulty in getting the right support is one of the main reasons that, for now, only coastal water shallower than 98 ft (30 m) is suitable for offshore developments.

THE ARGUMENT: Offshore wind power is better than onshore

For:
- Wind at the sea surface is stronger and fluctuates less than above land. This means towers can be shorter.
- There is more space offshore than onshore, so rotors can be bigger and generate more electricity.
- The oceans are flatter than most land, so there is less turbulence.

Against:
- It costs up to twice as much to put up a turbine in oceanic water as it does on land, because underwater construction costs are high. Costs increase with water depth.
- Turbines are farther away from where their power is needed, and it costs more to lay submarine cables to take electricity ashore.

CHAPTER 4 Living with wind power

Giant wind turbines are difficult to ignore, and they inspire mixed feelings in the people who regularly see or live with them. Objectors think they spoil the landscape, but for others, they are a symbol of clean energy. What are the pros and cons?

Visible energy

Onshore turbines work best when they are sited on high, windy ground, ideally on hilltops or cliffs, so that the wind blows toward them. They also work better on higher towers, because this holds the blades at an altitude where there is less turbulence in the air, and because the rotors are farther away from the land's rough surface. These factors mean that wind turbines are usually built in the countryside and are often visible from far away.

Although wind turbines are very tall, individual turbines take up only a relatively small amount of land. This means that the ground below can still be used, for example, by farmers who can graze livestock or grow crops right up to the base of the towers. On the other hand, there need to be many turbines in an area to provide as much electricity as a power station, so a wind farm probably covers more total land area per kilowatt produced.

People and tourism

Most turbines are sited in wild, windy, remote locations, away from major settlements. However, wind farms and

THE ARGUMENT: Turbines do not ruin the countryside

For:
- The landscape has already been altered substantially by human activity, such as farming, roads, and electricity pylons—so why pick on wind turbines?
- Turbines attract visitors interested in renewable energy and answers to the energy crisis.
- Farming can continue around wind turbines.

Against:
- People living near wind turbines say they find it almost impossible to sell their homes, because buyers do not like the turbines.
- With an expanding population, there is a great need to protect the remaining natural landscape and keep it turbine-free.

their visitor centers, where people can learn more about wind energy, can attract tourists to an area. Many people find wind turbines interesting and attractive. Critics, however, say that the turbines are unsightly and spoil landscapes, thereby reducing tourism to natural beauty spots. They claim that this has a negative effect on rural communities where tourism brings valuable revenue to people who work in local hotels, shops, and restaurants, for example.

▽ These hills, now dotted with wind turbines, were once covered in woodland that was long ago cleared for farming.

CASE STUDY: Attitude survey

In 2002, MORI—a U.K. organization that takes public opinion polls—did a survey of attitudes toward wind power among visitors to Scottish beauty spots. They found that 55 percent of tourists said that turbines generally or completely had a positive effect on their impression of Argyll beauty spots, 32 percent were ambivalent, and 8 percent said they gave a negative impression.

Wind turbines and wildlife

In general, wind power is good for the environment. Making materials for blades and other turbine parts causes some pollution, but once they are operating, they provide clean power. However, turbine blades swooshing through the air can harm flying

△ If these migrating birds flew any lower, the turbine blades would become a danger.

wildlife. Some scientists have reported high levels of wildlife death at wind farms. Some of the best sites for wind farms are in places where rare bird species live and breed. For example,

CASE STUDY: Ignoring advice about eagles

Today, any new wind farm has a legal obligation to protect wildlife. But sometimes power companies still site turbines where scientists say they should not be. Norway is home to most of the rare white-tailed eagles alive in the world. In 2005, a new wind farm was built on small islands where a major eagle population lived.

The bird charity RSPB had suggested that the turbines could harm these birds. By 2006, turbine blades had killed all three chicks from the previous year, plus many adults. Norway's plans to build further wind farms in different places could bring this species to the brink of extinction, unless better care on siting turbines is taken.

many endangered birds of prey are fatally injured or even chopped up by turbine blades in the Pyrenees, Spain, which is a major migration route for birds between Europe and Africa. Offshore wind farms may attract tired migrant birds looking for somewhere to rest. This is most likely at night when turbines are lit up to warn boats they are there. Whatever the actual danger to birds from turbines, most people agree it is much lower than that caused by cats and cars.

> ❝ The development of any form of energy, renewable or otherwise, must not compromise nature conservation objectives. ❞
>
> RSPB, *Wind farms and birds*, 2005, U.K.

In defense

Many wind farm operators claim that birds and bats usually sense and avoid turbines. They say that blades on modern turbines move too slowly to harm these animals anyway, and that power lines, used by various different generating methods, injure many more. Some turbines even create wildlife homes. For example, towers at offshore wind farms provide fixing points for seaweed, among which young fish and other animals are able to shelter and feed.

THE ARGUMENT: Turbines are good for wildlife

For:
- Preventing climate change is the best thing for wildlife.
- Offshore turbine towers can encourage wildlife.
- Wind farm operators follow regulations and use scientific advice to protect wildlife.
- Many rotor blades move too slowly to harm flying wildlife.

Against:
- Some evidence suggests that turbine blades have the potential to kill and injure flying animals, including birds and bats.
- Building offshore wind farms in shallow waters may damage breeding grounds for wildlife.
- Some wind farm locations are on migration routes and breeding sites for rare or threatened wildlife.

Turbine noise and health

In recent years, there has been some debate over whether turbines have a damaging effect on human health. One of the causes of this concern is noise. Wind turbines make two kinds of noise. Blades moving through air produce a "swishing" sound, and the faster or bigger the blades, the louder the sound. Some wind turbines also make a humming or whining noise, caused by mechanical parts in the gearbox and generator moving against each other. Some people have complained that these noises interrupt their sleep and cause stress, nausea, dizziness, and headaches.

Turbine makers say that soundproofed gearboxes and more aerodynamic blades have greatly reduced turbine noise. Wind farms are usually built so far from homes that some of their noise is masked by other background sounds, such as rustling leaves.

Relative noise levels

The noise wind farms produce is about the same level as you would hear from a nearby fast-flowing stream. The British Wind Energy Association states the sound power level of a wind farm 1,150 ft (350 m) away as a level 45, and compares that to the sound level of a quiet bedroom (35), a car driving at 40 mph (65 kph) 330 ft (100 m) away (55), and a busy office (60).

Shadow flicker

When turbine blades rotate with the Sun behind them, especially at dawn or dusk, they cast flickering shadows below. Some people describe this as a flashing or strobe effect in their homes that is hard to block out, even with curtains. This is not only annoying, but it can also cause nausea or loss of balance. The strobe effect can even provoke seizures (fits) in people with epilepsy. In the future, experts intend to use computer programs to predict shadow-casting patterns, so that turbines can be positioned without the flickering affecting local people.

> **" I compare the noise to Chinese water torture or fingernails on a chalkboard; windows closed, pillows over the head, it is still inescapable. "**
>
> Linda Cooper, wind farm neighbor, West Virginia

> **" We had been told they were ugly and noisy. Wrong—they are quiet and look far better than pylons. "**
>
> Malcolm McInnes Fareham, 1994 visitor to Delabole Wind Farm, U.K.

△ This protestor feels strongly that turbines will spoil the remote, quiet landscape of the Isle of Lewis, Scotland.

CASE STUDY: Taking action

In some places, groups of residents living near proposed wind farm sites are forming action groups to campaign against their construction on the grounds of health. By working as a group, their voice is heard more than individuals'. MAIWAG stands for Marton, Askam, and Ireleth Windfarm Action Group, and was formed by people from three villages in Cumbria, in northern England, who are fighting to prevent the local building of additional wind farms. Those who support the new turbines accuse protesters of being NIMBY. This stands for Not In My Back Yard—objecting to something in their own neighborhood, but not when it is built elsewhere. Supporters ask how would the protesters rather make their electricity?

Turbine hazards

A modern wind turbine, designed to last about 20 years, will operate for over 100,000 hours during its lifetime, and will have to cope with some extreme weather. Fast winds have several effects on turbines. Turbine blades, even those with carefully tested designs, can bend and snap, especially if their structure has weakened after many years of operation in varying conditions. Damaged rotors can make whole turbines become unstable and topple. The blades and shaft move so fast that friction inside the gearbox

△ Maintenance engineers check nacelles, hubs, and blades, using climbing harnesses and ropes to remain safe at work.

and generator can cause overheating or even fire. Other extreme weather, such as lightning strikes during electrical storms, can also damage these tall structures.

Safety measures

Wind turbine makers say that turbine safety features prevent accidents. Strong brakes automatically slow the rotor down as winds get stronger, to keep the shaft and generator turning at the right speed. The brakes stop the rotor completely when winds blow faster than 82 ft/s (25 m/s), at which speed blade tips are traveling at hundreds of miles per hour. Sensors in nacelles can detect excessive vibrations that might signal turbine failure and will switch off turbines. Manufacturers also state that many turbines are sited in remote places or offshore where few people live, and that turbines are regularly inspected for safety. What is more, compared to other power source safety records, wind is virtually harmless. For example, at least 6,000 miners die each year in China from mining coal for power stations.

When turbines fail

Some turbine accidents happen each year and not just in extreme winds. Whenever brake systems fail, because of power outages, for example, blades can move too fast, causing nacelle fires and blade damage. In the case of giant turbines, there is very little that firefighters with normal ladders and hoses can do to exinguish a blaze in a nacelle 196 feet (60 meters) in the air.

Broken blades do not just drop off—they can fly for a quarter-mile from the tower. In 2002 in Germany, a whole turbine that weighed over 110 tons collapsed when it snapped from its concrete foundations—a result of poor construction. Although there have been no fatalities for people yet, some turbines are sited near roads and are a potential danger.

THE ARGUMENT: Wind turbines are a safe option

For:
- Wind power is much safer in general than many other forms of power, such as nuclear power.
- Turbines have lots of inbuilt safety features.
- Extreme winds and lightning can damage all sorts of structures, not just turbines.

Against:
- Turbine parts and safety systems do occasionally fail, causing accidents each year.
- Testing in a laboratory is not the same as operating in variable weather conditions over long periods, so the safety of new, bigger turbines is uncertain.
- Increasing use of wind power may produce fatalities, as more turbines are sited close to settlements.

CHAPTER 5 The economics of wind power

Most wind turbines feed the electricity they generate directly into the power grid. However, debates continue as to whether wind power is reliable, cost-effective, or productive enough to have an impact compared with other power sources.

THE ARGUMENT:
Wind power is reliable

For:
- Most variations in output from wind farms can be compensated for by storing electricity or topping up supply from the grid.

- No power sources operate nonstop —nuclear plants often have sudden shutdowns for repairs.

Against:
- Wind power cannot produce electricity 24 hours a day like fossil fuel power stations.

- Many wind turbines operate at only 25–50 percent of their capacity most of the time due to varying wind energy.

Supply and demand
Most people know that winds can change direction suddenly, and that there may be a howling gale one day and no breeze at all the next. Even in the windiest places, wind does not blow all the time, so wind power fluctuates. This can be a big problem when wind is the only power supply, but less so when the turbines are connected to a grid. Then electricity from other sources can fulfill demand when wind energy is at its lowest.

However, some aspects of wind are predictable. In general, winds are stronger by day than they are by night, and in temperate zones, such as Europe and North America, winds are stronger in the winter than they are in the summer. On the whole, these weather patterns correspond with the ebb and flow of electricity demands. For example, more electricity is used for heat and light in the winter, when it is colder and darker, than in the summer. More electricity is used during the day, for example, in offices and schools, than at night, when most people are asleep.

Supplements and solutions
There are ways of coping with the ups and downs of wind energy supplies.

One way is to store excess electricity during periods of strong wind in large batteries. The downsides of this are that the process of manufacturing batteries causes pollution, and they do not store electricity well for long periods (although storage technology should improve in time).

Another practical solution is local or international cooperation. For example, Denmark often has excess wind power and at some times of the year, Norway has an excess of water power—so by linking national grids, there might be a way of providing a constant supply for both countries. In the case of microgeneration systems (see page 18), some owners may be able to sell excess power to local electricity companies if they are connected to the grid, so that they can afford to buy electricity from other sources when they need to.

▽ Although many industries shut down at night, domestic demand for electricity often increases at night when there is less wind.

Starting up wind power

Any power plant costs a lot of money to set up—a price that is paid back during its lifetime as electricity is sold. The cost of installing wind power is an average of about $1,000 per kilowatt. Bigger wind farms cost more to set up, because more cabling and more land is required. However, it takes a certain amount of ground and construction expense to put up any turbine, regardless of size.

Developers do not always have the money they need to set up a wind power project. They can borrow money from banks, such as the World Bank, and pay it back with interest over the lifetime of the farm. They may also get grants from charities and governments anxious to promote wind power. Sometimes, individuals group together to raise funds. However, private energy companies are often the main funders of wind power, and make money by selling it back in time.

The price of wind

The costs of running wind turbines after setup are low. No fuel needs to be bought, operating costs are small, there is no pollution to clear up, and they are cheap to take down at the end of their lives. This compares with, say, nuclear power stations, which have ongoing costs of fuel that fluctuate with world market prices, and dangerous waste disposal throughout and beyond the lifetime of a reactor.

In the 1980s, when the first large turbines feeding into the electricity grid were set up, wind power cost 30 cents per kilowatt hour. Today, the cost is closer to a fifth of this for new, large wind farms. This makes large-scale wind power comparable in cost to new fossil fuel and hydropower plants, although small-scale wind power is still more expensive. However, the actual price of power alternatives is rarely compared fairly. For example, it is estimated that electricity from coal-fired power stations would be three times more expensive than wind power if the cost of clearing up environmental pollution was included.

> **"** If it is just a big company doing a wind farm, the community doesn't feel it owns it. And then they will resist. And once you encounter resistance, you are going to have to work harder and harder against the negativity. **"**
>
> Jens Larsen, Middelgrunden developer, Denmark

△ The offshore turbines at Middelgrunden wind farm in Denmark were built after taking the views of local people into consideration.

CASE STUDY:
A cooperative wind farm in Denmark

Sometimes people come together to help make wind power happen. Middelgrunden cooperative is a Danish organization, formed by the Copenhagen municipal electricity company and more than 8,000 local people in an environmental group. The group was involved in the planning stages for an offshore wind farm near Copenhagen, and was able to voice its specific concerns. When it was satisfied with the design, the group raised half of the funds needed to develop the farm by selling shares in the cooperative. Each share cost around $750 and entitles its owner to the money made from selling 1 MW per year in the future. By selling shares, the wind farm is now working and returning the shareholders' investments in renewable energy.

Global pressure for wind

Many countries worldwide are trying to encourage wind power schemes. This is partly because wind power is now more economic than ever before. It is also partly out of necessity as fossil fuel stocks dwindle and cost more. Companies such as Shell, purely an oil and gas company in the past, are now investing in wind power, too. There is also the issue of security. For example, political instability in the Middle East, where most of the world's oil comes from, could affect future oil supplies for many countries. Also, large power stations—especially nuclear—may be seen as potential terrorist targets. Smaller amounts of electricity from lots of turbines should remain a secure source of power.

The United Nations held an Earth Summit in 1982, where most countries in the world agreed that greenhouse gas emissions should be severely reduced to slow global warming. At a follow-up meeting in 1996, in Kyoto, Japan, 163 countries agreed on targets

▽ Most scientists accept that polar ice cover is shrinking due to global warming, which is gradually causing sea levels to rise.

for cutting global emissions by 5 percent compared to 1990 levels by 2012. This was called the *Kyoto protocol*. One problem was that two of the biggest polluters in the world—the United States and China—refused to agree to the protocol. However, many individual countries, including the U.S., have established their own targets, and are promoting wind power along with other renewables.

Laws and subsidies

Some countries are making it easier to put up wind turbines by changing laws. For example, in the U.K. in 2006, the government decided that home-owners no longer needed special planning permission from local councils to put up turbines or solar panels.

> **"** It is patently absurd that you should be able to put up a satellite dish on your house, but have to wrestle with the planning process for small-scale microgeneration, which is no more obtrusive and can have real impact on tackling climate change. **"**
>
> Yvette Cooper, Planning Minister, U.K.

This positive change could make microgeneration projects much more widespread in the future. Other countries, such as Germany, have used subsidies to encourage renewables. These are payments that governments or other groups contribute toward the high cost of setting up turbines.

THE ARGUMENT: Governments should subsidize wind power

For:

- Any encouragement of renewable energy is good, because it reduces greenhouse gases.
- Subsidizing wind is fair, because other power sources were, or still are, being subsidized.

Against:

- People want cheap power, whatever its source. By subsidizing wind power, governments are admitting it is too expensive and making taxpayers pay too much for their electricity.
- Some power companies might start wind projects just to get subsidies, and not because they have a commitment to alternative energy.

CHAPTER 6

Wind power now and in the future

There are many possible growth areas for wind power, and future technology may well affect the importance of this resource in the energy mix. To look after the Earth, and also to prevent energy wastage, people need to use more renewables.

Wind power today

Within the last 15 years, more wind farms have been constructed in more countries around the world than ever before. Although presently, wind energy fulfills less than 0.02 percent of the world's total power needs, there are already around 40,000 turbines distributed among 40 countries—and this number of turbines is increasing by about 25 percent each year.

The location of wind turbines varies. Some countries, such as Denmark, which produces one-tenth of its electricity needs through wind power,

▽ Using wind power in LEDCs, such as India, should reduce the amount of wood local people have to cut and burn for heat and cooking.

have a significant green commitment. They, like the world leader in the wind power league table, Germany, are choosing to develop wind power because they see it as an environmentally friendly option. For countries such as Spain, there is the added incentive that they have steady winds, straight off the Atlantic ocean, and therefore a reliable source of power. Wind turbine installations in some other countries, such as India, are being built because wind power is a cheap alternative to extending the grid to remote or underdeveloped areas.

> If there is an area that is of utmost importance for our future, that area is renewable energy.

Jose Socrates, Prime Minister of Portugal, 2005

Growth areas

The use of wind power is increasing in regions such as Central Asia and China, where there are regular strong winds and numerous suitable windy locations. The United Kingdom and Ireland are also likely growth areas, because they lie next to the Atlantic ocean, which experiences high winds.

Many governments have set targets for increasing the number of wind farms in their countries, often as a result of pressure from the public. Germany plans to source one-quarter of all its electricity needs from wind power within the next 25 years, and Portugal wants to double the contribution wind power makes to its national grid.

CASE STUDY: Power to Portugal

In 2006, Portugal launched a project to double its wind power capacity and use turbines to provide enough electricity for 750,000 homes. Portugal's coastline, over 500 miles (800 kilometers) long, regularly feels the full force of Atlantic winds, and 500 new turbines will be built at various locations along it to take advantage of this natural energy source. The country's new wind power project runs alongside expanding solar and wave power systems. The government hopes that these schemes combined will work to help meet targets set by the Kyoto protocol and significantly reduce greenhouse gas emissions by the year 2012.

Technical innovation

The turbines of the future may differ slightly from those of today. Designers and engineers are developing new types that generate more efficiently in slow winds. The quietrevolution, for example, is a VAWT (see page 15) that stands around 16 feet (5 meters) high, excluding the pole or tower. It has three spiral-shaped blades and can generate enough electricity from gentle winds of 20 feet (6 meters) per second to power five energy-efficient homes. When computer-controlled lights are set on the fast-spinning blades of this turbine, they can produce patterns so that at night, the machine doubles up as art, advertising billboards, or even a flag display. This turbine is ideal for urban settings with limited space.

Other designs could increase the power output per turbine from moderate wind resources. Shrouded turbines are HAWTs (see page 14) with a funnel-shaped duct in front of the rotor to focus and speed up the moving air against the blades. This works well in theory, but in practice the duct causes turbulence, and even directs wind away from the blades.

◁ Quietrevolution's tapered, S-shaped blades make it turn silently in winds from any direction. The small generator is at the base of the blades, on the main shaft.

> **"** City dwellers and businesses are the biggest users of energy, but ironically, the impact of wind generation has been traditionally focused on rural areas—the area where least energy is consumed. [Harnessing urban wind] brings the debate on wind generation directly into the cities. **"**
>
> Robert Webb, chief executive officer, Quiet Revolution Ltd, U.K.

Another approach is counterrotating turbines. These have two rotors working in opposite directions. Designers claim these should provide one-third more power than standard turbines, but at anything other than ideal wind speeds and direction, turbulence makes the blades vibrate too much as they pass each other.

New settings

It may be that in the future, people microgenerate more of their own power rather than relying on grids, even in urban settings. Ducted turbines are already in operation on some tall buildings. These have slots that capture updrafts of air up the sides of the building and direct it over covered turbines. In the future, wind power may be drawn from higher up in the atmosphere where wind resources are stronger. One idea is to suspend turbines hundreds of feet above the ground from large balloons, which are tied to the Earth using strong power cables.

CASE STUDY: An eco-city in China

A sustainable city is being built on an island in the Yangtze river, near Shanghai, China. City planners have designed this self-sufficient settlement of 500,000 people in response to the growing pollution and overcrowding in Chinese cities. Dontang eco-city will have lots of green spaces and farmland to grow food for its residents. Transportation will be by bicycle or public vehicles. Houses built along canals will have turbines, such as the quietrevolution, and solar cells to provide much of their power. In the future, this could be a model for many settlements worldwide.

> **❝** There isn't any energy crisis. It's simply a crisis of ignorance. **❞**
>
> Buckminster Fuller, U.S. architect, designer, and writer

Facing the energy crisis

Every year, people around the world are using more and more energy. One reason for this is a growing population; the other is an increase in the standard of living—the quality and quantity of goods and services available to people—that is occurring. At current rates of growth, there is no way that today's power plants will be able to cope with future demand. There are two ways to respond to an energy crisis of this kind—to increase the number and efficiency of power sources, and to reduce the amount of energy people use in the first place.

◁ There are huge energy savings to be made by building new houses with very thick insulation to stop heat from escaping. Typically, they need only about a quarter of the electricity normal houses need to stay warm.

Increasing energy supply

Increasing efficiency, as oil companies are doing by reducing the amount of oil wasted through spillages and leaks, can boost energy supplies. However, increasing power sources is more complicated. Most people agree that renewable energy is best for the planet, but it is unlikely that one source, such as wind power, would be able to supply all the world needs. For example, in Germany, demand is currently rising 70 times faster than the wind energy production. Countries are now debating what kind of energy mix they will be using in the future.

Most governments rest their hopes on a combination of renewables, such as solar, wave, and wind power, along with fossil fuel or nuclear technologies. Or could the answer lie with hydrogen power? There is a potentially limitless supply of this gas, which can be obtained from renewable resources and used to create "clean" fuel cells. If wind power provided the electricity needed to create hydrogen fuel, it would be nonpolluting.

Saving energy

There are many things individuals, companies, and governments can do to save energy. Reducing waste—for example, by switching off appliances rather than leaving them on standby—is one action. Fitting double-glazing and loft insulation, and buying low-energy versions of appliances, such as freezers and light bulbs, are others. Reduced energy use would mean that renewable technologies, such as wind power, would be able to supply a bigger percentage of the world's electricity, and it would also reduce carbon emissions and air pollution.

CASE STUDY: Insulation or generation?

A recent study by Pilkington Insulation Company, in the U.K., made some calculations to find out which saved more energy and reduced pollution more—building wind turbines, or insulating houses? They figured out that by insulating 485 houses, they could save the amount of energy output each year by a 750-kW turbine. When they factored in the relative installation costs, they discovered that insulation is 55 times more effective at reducing energy use and pollution than wind power. Ideally, people in the future will insulate and also use power generated by wind and other renewable sources of energy.

Tomorrow's power

It is true that wind cannot meet all the world's round-the-clock energy needs. Like solar technology, it would have to be supplemented by additional power supplies, such as those from fossil fuel power plants or from other renewable resources. But the potential of wind power to play a significant role in energy production—particularly as technological advances make turbines more efficient and cheaper—is great. Scientists have calculated that the energy in the world's winds could provide twice the expected global power demand in 2020.

Building enough turbines would require lots more space, with wind farms covering giant areas of upland and shallow sea. The implications for people's health and livelihoods, the environment, and landscapes would be immense. What is more, wind is a variable resource across the globe. Some parts of the world cannot get the power they need from wind using today's turbines, power storage, and supply systems. However, many of the fastest-growing cities are at, or near, the coast and could be powered by strong offshore winds.

The position of wind in the energy mix is uncertain. It is likely to have a significant place alongside solar power and hydropower. Its importance will be determined not only by power companies, who must balance the need to make money by supplying cheap power against their environmental responsibilities, but it will also be shaped by the political will of governments, who can encourage or

THE ARGUMENT:
Wind energy will power the future

For:
- Wind is a free, renewable resource that produces zero pollution.
- Costs of turbines are falling as they become more efficient.
- Wind generally blows strongest at the times of year when power is needed most.

Against:
- Wind resources are intermittent and vary across the world.
- Turbines cost a lot to set up, making their power no cheaper than other sources.
- Some people believe that wind turbines spoil landscapes and pose a danger to human health, and that they may also harm wildlife.

discourage wind power through taxes, laws, and regulations. Governments are expected to listen to the needs and opinions of their citizens. So, the more people support and invest in wind power, the more likely governments will be to promote and subsidize it.

Changing climate

Increasing the power we attain from renewables is a major way to address climate change. Even if just 10 percent of the world's power was supplied by wind, the atmosphere would be spared one-sixth of all CO_2 emissions. But how will a changing climate affect winds? Will wind speeds and directions alter as the world gets warmer? Whatever happens, the present rise in energy demand is much faster than any renewables or new fuel can provide. The most important way to address our current energy crisis is to use less.

▽ The changing world climate is causing shifts in wind patterns that could impact wind power in future.

Glossary

Acid rain Rainwater that has been changed when gases in the air dissolve in it. Acid rain is damaging to plants, animals, and stone buildings.

Aerodynamic Streamlined and offering least resistance to air flow.

Altitude Height above sea level.

Atmosphere Layers of gases that surround the Earth.

Biogas Gas made when bacteria and other organisms rot organic material in oxygen-free conditions.

Blade The part of a wind turbine that is pushed by wind.

Electron A tiny particle within an atom. Electrons may cause other electrons to move, creating electricity.

Fossil fuel Natural fuel, such as oil, gas, and coal, which formed from the remains of living things trapped in layers of rock millions of years ago.

Gearbox The machine that transmits power and changes the rotation speed from a turbine or motor, to another device, such as wheels or a generator.

Generator A machine that transforms rotational energy into electrical energy.

Global warming The general, gradual rise in average temperature around the world, caused by greenhouse gases.

Greenhouse gas An atmospheric gas that traps the Sun's heat reflecting off the Earth, raising temperatures.

Grid The network of power lines.

Hub The part of a turbine that the blades attach to, which turns the shaft.

Hydropower The electricity that is generated when falling fresh water turns turbines.

Nacelle The part of a wind turbine that houses its mechanical parts.

Nonrenewable An energy source that is in limited supply and will run out one day, such as coal, oil, and gas.

Nuclear power Electricity made by heating water using energy from within atoms (microscopic particles).

Power outage When the grid is damaged, or generating machinery is not working, so there is no electricity.

Renewable An energy source that is in limitless supply, such as wind, moving water, and sunlight.

Rotor A hub with blades.

Temperate Regions of the world with distinct hot and cold seasons.

Topography The shape or surface features of the land.

Trade winds Cool winds that blow from north or south toward the equator.

Turbulence Changes in wind direction and speed, often caused by obstacles.

Wind shade The area around a wind turbine where turbulence causes especially low wind speed.

Books to read

Choosing Windpower Hugh Piggott, Centre for Alternative Technology, Powys 2006: outlines how and where to use wind power for microgeneration.

Energy Essentials: Renewable Energy Nigel Saunders and Steven Chapman, Raintree, Oxford 2005: shows the energy crisis and its many possible solutions.

Looking At Energy: Wind Power Polly Goodman, Wayland, London, 2005: looks at ways people use wind, including wind-powered ocean oil tankers.

Renewable Energy Resources Trevor Smith, Smart Apple Media, Mankato, 2004: explores global options for using renewables in the energy mix.

Web Sites

Due to the changing nature of Internet links, The Rosen Publishing Group, Inc., has developed an online list of Web sites related to the subject of this book. This site is updated regularly. Please use this link to access the list:
www.rosenlinks.com/ted/wind/

Note: Page numbers in *italic* refer to illustrations.